Leadership and Self Deception:

Maximise your potential for a successful life in 5 steps

By Thomas Garry

Description

Do you want to regain your self-esteem and give a boost to your life? Have you ever found yourself wishing that you had it in you to take charge of a situation? You can become the leader of your own life with the tactics and suggestions found in this book. It is now time to discover a multitude of practical, applicable techniques for consciously boosting your self-esteem. From how to act more assertively to practicing self-love, the way that you go through life will change for the better once you implement these five steps!

Today's demanding work environment can be extremely frustrating and challenging, especially when you are failing to be the leader of your own life. However, you do not have to live according to somebody else's rules. With the right amount of dedication and diligence, you can transform the way that you think about yourself and take charge of your life. Going through life does not have to be a passive process and neither do your interpersonal interactions. Even if you are already pretty happy with your self-esteem, this book's content can be of great assistance to you. You might be shocked to discover that your favorite activities are damaging your self-esteem and ability to lead your own life. Self-esteem issues can develop at an extremely early age; learn how to overcome them.

5 Benefits of Leadership and self-deception: Maximise your potential for a successful life in 5 Steps

1. Learn the benefits of developing healthy self-esteem, as well as the consequences of failing to do so.
2. Discover methods for overcoming negative thought patterns that hamper self-esteem.
3. Utilize premeditated conversation tactics and patterns that will help you effectively assert yourself.
4. Read about the dangers that procrastinating poses to your self-esteem.
5. Self-esteem is essential to managing and directing your efforts towards your goals in life.

Curious to Learn More?

Download your copy of *Leadership and self-deception: Maximise your potential for a successful life in 5 Steps* today! Take control of the direction of your life!

Table of Contents

Introduction

Congratulations on downloading *Leadership and self-deception: Maximise your potential for a successful life in 5 Steps* and thank you for doing so. Self-esteem describes the feelings of worthiness and value that one assigns to themselves as a person. A multitude of factors affect one's self-esteem, including life circumstances and input from mentors and relatives.

Self-esteem development begins at a very early age. Researchers suggest that humans have the capacity to develop self-esteem as soon as they can recognize their own name. Problems with self-esteem start to occur when one or more needs fail to get fulfilled. Specifically, the needs for belongingness, attention, affirmation, safety, and love must be fulfilled in order for healthy self-esteem development to occur.

As humans start to undergo the lifelong process of socialization, they realize that a degree of power to have these needs met lies in their hands. So, when one of these essential needs is not met, one might blame themselves, which leads to reductions in self-esteem. For example, when a peer group intentionally excludes a single child on the schoolyard, that child may believe that his rejection has something to do with his own shortcomings. The socialization process dictates that the excluded child will learn from the experience, and either find a new peer group or make adjustments to the ways in which he goes about making friends. However, if enough of these rejections occur over a period of time, that child will begin to think that he must be worth less than those who reject him. In his mind, if he were a person worth being friends with, then the other children would automatically accept him into their social circle.

Your current level of self-esteem is a product of a lifetime of receiving messages relating to your personal qualities. To illustrate, imagine that, as a child, you interrupted your mom while she was speaking on the phone. The way in which she responded to your interruption had a lasting impact on your self-esteem. Did she tell you that your behavior was rude, or that *you* were rude? In the event that you were informed that your behavior was rude, you would have gotten the idea that you can make adjustments to your actions in the future to avoid upsetting your mother. On the other hand, if you were told that you yourself are rude, then you would be led to believe that you lack the power to do anything about your behavior in the future. Being rude, according to this belief system, is just a part of who you are; you cannot help that you are like that. Thankfully, you can take steps today to undo the effects that a lifetime of harming messages had on your self-esteem.

If you go through your own life with an ingrained belief that you are a bad person, then you will struggle with self-esteem. You will believe that anything good that you experience is a fluke. You will believe that, because you are a bad person, you deserve for bad things to happen to you.

Building self-esteem is challenging and rewarding. Convincing somebody that they have a lot of value as a person when they have been led to believe otherwise for the majority of their life often proves highly difficult. This challenge is akin to convincing somebody that what they believe to be the color purple is instead, in fact, actually orange.

In addition, low self-esteem can develop as a strategy for coping with anxiety that was caused by feelings of inadequacy during one's early life. In other words, if people blames themselves for all bad things in their life, then they do not have to experience the uncomfortable confrontations and conflicts that they are too anxious to engage in.

This book will help readers develop the self-esteem that they rightfully deserve to carry with them at all times. Readers can expect to become the leaders of their own lives if they diligently work at repairing their self-esteem. The following chapters will discuss a five-step process for building a solid foundation of self-esteem and consciously taking charge of the value that you assign to yourself. Chapter 1 outlines the importance of having high self-esteem, detailing the side effects of both high and low self-esteem. Chapter 2 provides strategies for adopting a more positive perspective, something critical to the development of self-esteem. Chapter 3 outlines the self-love tactics that will contribute to higher levels of self-esteem. In chapter 4, readers can expect to learn about how to assert oneself appropriately, something that people with high self-esteem do. Finally, chapter 5 lists behaviors that one must avoid if self-esteem is to be built. You possess the power to regain your self-esteem and become the leader of your own life. Action and a willingness to engage with new ideas are essential to the success of your journey.

The 5-step process outlined in this book is not published in any particular order. Start your journey with the processes and strategies that feel most comfortable to you, and then make your way towards implementing the rest of the book's suggestions.

The market contains a large plethora of publications concerning this subject. Thanks again for choosing this one! Every effort was made to ensure that this book is as full of as much useful information as possible. Please enjoy!

Chapter 1: Step 1 – Understanding Self-Esteem's Importance

High and low levels of self-esteem manifest a number of visible symptoms. When a person has a high quantity of self-esteem, they tend to display a large amount of attractive traits. On the other hand, low or negative levels of self-esteem will manifest themselves in a series of unattractive symptoms within the person with low self-esteem. Actively taking steps to boost your self-esteem will give you advantages that you previously did not get to enjoy.

High Self-Esteem

People who possess high levels of self-esteem demonstrate it, usually subconsciously, through a series of traits and behaviors that others find attractive. To illustrate, studies demonstrate that people who value themselves highly are good at self-direction, have a forgiving nature, think optimistically, care for themselves, are able to trust other people, behave independently, seek cooperation, feel comfortable experiencing strong and widely varying emotions, possess confidence, believe in their own personal strengths, refuse to be manipulated, are aware of the limits of their abilities, and are aware of their own unique strengths.

First and foremost, individuals with healthy amounts of self-esteem are strong at directing themselves. In other words, they lead their own lives. Self-direction is the act of taking initiative and guiding oneself towards their own healthy goals. Self-directed people do not rely on prompts from others in order to start making progress. They act according to their own beliefs concerning what they want out of life. People who possess high levels of self-direction are proactive in that they take it upon themselves to make the most of their time. They do not sit around and wait for inspiration to strike. They are motivated by their own successes. They go about their work trying to earn the things that they truly want, not the things that they believe that they "should" have. High self-esteem will contribute to a better sense of self-direction. On the other hand, self-destruction is the opposite of self-direction. Self-destructive people stand in the way of their own achievements.

As an example, imagine that you want to stop working at your current place of employment. In other words, you want to quit. In this situation, a self-directed person would actively seek employment elsewhere before they inform their superiors of their desire to leave the company. (Unless, of course, they can afford not to work.) They autonomously take actions that will set them up for success and a more enjoyable occupation. Conversely, a self-destructive person will wallow over the fact that they hate their work, blame the world for their inability to pay bills without enduring a miserable day job, all the while failing to seek better work elsewhere.

Second, high self-esteem levels contribute towards a forgiving nature. People who have healthy amounts of self-esteem forgive others, as well as themselves. Mistakes happen, and people with high self-esteem recognize and accept that. If you take it upon yourself to boost your self-esteem, you will be less likely to get frustrated with others when they make an honest mistake. In addition, you will be more likely to learn from your own mistakes. People with good self-esteem do not like to dwell on the setbacks that their mistakes cause. Instead, they learn from the experience, figure out what needs to be done in order to move past it, and take care to avoid making that very same mistake and ones like it in the future.

Third, by boosting your self-esteem, you stand to adopt a more optimistic way of thinking. Optimism leads to a more positive thought process concerning a variety of different situations and scenarios. When optimistic people experience a setback, they refuse to give up. They will start strategizing on how to overcome it. Optimistic people perceive images in a more positive manner as well. For example, one person might view a photograph of a woman shouting and believe that she is angry and out of control. An optimistic person can look at that very same image and think about how passionate and involved that woman looks. When something good happens to an optimist, they take responsibility for it and do not try to blow it off as a fluke. For example, if an optimist gets promoted at work, they will contribute their advancement to their own hard work and loyalty. In addition, optimists tend to experience more fulfilling relationships, including familial, romantic, and platonic. This is because they seek out other positive-thinking, fun individuals to interact with. They do not want a negative pessimist to lower their mood.

Fourth, people with high self-esteem take better care of themselves. They believe that the effort required to maintain a healthy lifestyle is worth the benefits that they will enjoy. Those enjoyable benefits are well deserved and worth working for, in their minds. Individuals who have healthy levels of self-esteem have an easier time practicing good hygiene, keeping their home clean, maintaining physical health, caring for their mental health, eating properly, and staying financially stable. They work hard for those benefits because they want to, not because some external source told them that they have to.

Fifth, people with high self-esteem are abler to trust the right people. Trust issues arise in those without self-esteem. People who lack self-esteem cannot believe that somebody else would want to uphold a promise or keep a secret for them. High self-esteem individuals believe that they are worthy of other people's affections.

Sixth, those with a good sense of self-esteem act independently. They believe in their ability to take action without the approval of others. They do not wait for another person to validate their choices, nor do they need to. People with high self-esteem are the leaders of their own lives because they choose to be. They do not need permission from anyone else to do anything.

Seventh, possessors of high-self-esteem seek cooperation. Cooperation involves combining multiple people's efforts in order to achieve something greater than that which could have been achieved working solo. However, cooperation requires that cooperators trust their fellow collaborators to hold up their respective ends of the workload. Furthermore, cooperators must relinquish some element of control as they allow others to contribute to their projects. A healthy dose of self-esteem is required for relinquishing control to and trusting others.

Eight, those who have good self-esteem will feel relatively comfortable experiencing and expressing a wide range of emotions of various intensities. They believe that their emotions are valid and therefore okay to be felt and displayed. People with high self-esteem emote in healthy ways. Being in touch and comfortable with one's own emotions is a tell-tale sign of healthy self-esteem levels.

Ninth, if you have good self-esteem, you will possess confidence in yourself. Confidence is the feeling you get when you firmly believe in yourself. Confident people stand up for their convictions, go after what they want, socialize with ease, decisively make decisions, speak their mind when the situation calls for it, and take constructive criticism very well.

Tenth, those with high self-esteem believe in their own strengths. For example, a person learning a new language who has high self-esteem will know when they are ready to hold a conversation in the foreign tongue. On the other hand, a person without enough self-esteem will constantly doubt their ability to converse in their new language, constantly questioning whether they are "good enough" at said language.

Eleventh, people with good self-esteem refuse to be manipulated. They will not let another person pressure them into doing something that they do not want to do. They do not give others the chance the use them for personal gain.

Twelfth, people with high self-esteem have an acute awareness of their own abilities' limits. Furthermore, they are perfectly okay with their shortcomings. For example, you might not be able to bench press 150 pounds. If your self-esteem is high, you will be aware of the fact that you cannot attempt to lift that much weight without hurting yourself. Furthermore, you will be okay with your inability to press that weight. As such, you will not risk injury when you insist that you can in fact lift 150 pounds and proceed to throw your shoulder out trying. You know your limits and hold yourself to them.

Lastly, people with high self-esteem possess an accurate awareness of their own unique strengths. For example, a talented painter who has high self-esteem will know that they are good at painting. Such talents often reflect well on a resume. In the next chapter, you will learn a strategy for coming to realizations about the skills that you possess.

By taking it upon yourself to raise your self-esteem levels, you stand to live a more fulfilling life and develop more than a dozen concrete attractive personality traits.

Poor Self-Esteem

On the other hand, individuals with low, lacking levels of self-esteem display subconsciously a series of unattractive traits that indicate the lack of worthiness that they believe themselves to possess. To illustrate, people who suffer from low self-esteem think pessimistically, fear ridicule, fail to trust the right people, like to blame others for their shortcomings, feel like they cannot be loved, possess a perfectionist attitude, and have an irrational fear of risk. Unfortunately, the hampering effects that these symptoms place on one's quality of life often contribute to an even further lack of self-esteem.

First, people with low self-esteem have a tendency to take a pessimistic view on most things. Pessimism refers to a system of thoughts that take negative viewpoints. To illustrate, when a pessimist experiences a setback, they may give up on their goal altogether. For example, a pessimist trying to eat healthier may cave under stress and indulge in a donut. Instead of owning up to their slip-up and vowing to do better next time, they might give up on their diet altogether, losing faith in their ability to maintain a healthy lifestyle.

Second, individuals who have low self-esteem greatly fear ridicule. Ridicule shatters the fragile sense of value that they place on themselves. As such, this fear prevents them from trying in most cases. In their minds, they might as well not try, because, if they fail, then they might get ridiculed. Fear of ridicule can also prevent people from expressing valid opinions and sharing ideas.

Third, those with low self-esteem tend to have an underlying belief that they cannot be loved. They dwell on their shortcomings, so they assume that other people must do the same thing. Even when somebody shows a low self-esteem sufferer affection, the person afflicted with low self-esteem thinks that it is just a matter of time before the affectionate person discovers reasons not to love them. Relationships suffer as a result.

Fourth, individuals who suffer from low self-esteem possess a perfectionist attitude. They think that they must be perfect all the time, or else they will fall short of other people's expectations. Nothing except for their absolute best seems good enough. These people will frustrate themselves to no end trying to perfect every project, assignment, and task that somebody else will see. They have to display their very best and nothing else at all times, even if that means ignoring other responsibilities in order to devote oneself to a certain task.

Finally, people with low self-esteem possess a highly irrational, crippling fear of risk. Fear of failure prevents these people from taking risks. If you never try, you will never experience failure. People who do not take risks are doomed to a life of complacency.

Sadly, the effects that these self-defeating behaviors have on one's life and psyche cause more drops in self-esteem. The only way to defeat this downward spiral is to actively develop self-esteem through a series of concrete behavioral and attitudinal changes. The chapters that follow will guide you through this process. Self-esteem will give you the confidence necessary to guide your own life.

Chapter 2: Step 2 – Focus on the Positive

People with low self-esteem have a tendency to wallow in negativity. By focusing on the negative, you ignore large amounts of information that might otherwise make you feel better about yourself. Healthy self-esteem is the goal here. If you have struggled with self-esteem for some time, chances are that you often overlook the positive aspects of your life. Positivity is powerful; this chapter will provide suggestions for harnessing its powers in order to go through life with better self-esteem.

Positive Self-Talk

Self-talk is the interactions that you have with the voice that resides inside of your own mind. The things that this voice says greatly affect the way that you feel and think. As such, negative self-talk can lead to saddening thought patterns and a lack of self-esteem. Consequently, positive self-talk is an essential component in building up one's self-esteem.

Making the practice of positive self-talk a regular habit should be your ultimate goal in terms of self-talk outcomes. Practicing positive self-talk might feel unusual or funny when you first begin, but, after you start to benefit from its self-esteem boosting effects, you will yearn for the opportunity to engage in positive self-talk uninterrupted.

Positive self-talk does not necessarily involve pointing out the things that you wish to change. For example, you might tell yourself that you want to behave less erratically, experience fewer feelings of anxiety, and stop living in a messy apartment. However, the problem with these thoughts lies in the fact that they focus on what you would rather not have. Instead, positive self-talk should focus on the things and outcomes that you do indeed want.

Positive self-talk takes place in the present-tense and affirms the qualities that correlate with high self-esteem. For example, repeat to yourself affirmations like "I am assertive," "I can make as much money as I want to," and "I feel calm." Studies of propaganda techniques prove that the more a person is exposed to a message, the more strongly they will believe that message. So, repeating your positive self-talk messages to yourself regularly will lead to a solid belief in your abilities and positive traits, which, in turn, will lead to a better level of self-esteem.

A holistic approach to positive self-talk extends beyond repeating the aforementioned positive affirmations. It also includes the elimination of negative self-talk, the replacement of negative connections, and a dedication to living in the moment.

The elimination of negative self-talk is crucial to building self-esteem and leading one's own life. Negative self-talk takes the form of harsh unwarranted criticisms towards oneself. For example, a person engaged in such toxic self-loathing might tell themselves "I can never do anything right" or "I am weak." These harmful beliefs might stem from messages that were reinforced by sources of authority early on in life, such as a very serious gym teacher who criticizes students that are out of shape. Practice being aware of your negative self-talk. Your negative self-talk might be pointing out the things that you need to work on about yourself, but it could also be unduly harming your self-esteem. The next time you find yourself performing negative self-talk, question your own claims. For example, if you say to yourself "I cannot do this thing," ask yourself "Why can't I do this thing?" You just might struggle to find a good answer, which will in turn cause you to change the way you think about your abilities.

Next, you must eliminate negative connections from your life. Negative connections are the people that influence your thoughts in such a way that causes your thinking to negatively affect your quality of life and self-esteem. These people might never say anything bad about you, but the way that they think about the world will rub off on you. For example, if you have a roommate who constantly badmouths all of his professors, his regular criticisms of others will start to seem normal to you. You might pick up on his habits and start looking for faults in others as well.

Evolution dictates that humans adopt the majority of their social group's belief system. When humans lived in tribal societies, if your tribe considered your beliefs too extreme or contradictory, then you would be eliminated from your tribe. At this point, your only options would be to gain acceptance in another tribe, or start your own tribe and convince other outcasts to join it. If you failed to do either of those things, then you would die, as tribe members depended on one another for continued survival. Of course, chances are that you do not live in a tribe, but the evolutionary mechanism that causes humans to take on the thought patterns of their social group still exists within the human psyche. It is an outdated, obsolete behavior that, many thousands of years ago, aided with human survival. However, you still must contend with its existence. You will adopt the thought patterns of the people that you choose to surround yourself with; make sure to include as many positive-thinking individuals in your life as you can. Simultaneously cut ties with those who think primarily negative or toxic thoughts.

Moving along, positive self-talk would not be complete without a dedication to living in the moment. People with high self-esteem do not let anxiety related to their future stop them from enjoying life. Instead, if a hindering issue arises, they handle their worries. They tell themselves that they can take steps to overcome problems right now, and then follow up. Furthermore, they focus their thoughts on positive experiences. When an enjoyable happening takes place in your life, take a moment to appreciate it. Then, in the event that you find yourself experiencing unpleasant or negative self-talk, bring yourself back to that wonderful moment. Remembering happy times will greatly help your self-esteem levels, as well as your overall happiness and feelings of fulfillment.

Think Positively

Negative thinking is toxic. Positive thoughts will make you happier and feel more in control of your own life. When you view the world as a happy place full of opportunity, you stand to behave in accordance with your beliefs; you will go through life with a sense of direction.

Celebrate Successes

Inevitably, if you take any kind of risks during your lifetime, you will do some things well and other tasks poorly. It is important for your self-esteem that you recognize what you do well. It does not matter how seemingly insignificant your successes appear; you should praise yourself for having achieved them. For example, if your dedication and loyalty to your place of employment earned you a fifteen cent hourly raise, take some time to pat yourself on the back. Your boss recognized your hard work and you should too.

If you have struggled with self-esteem issues for a period of time, you might have trouble recognizing successes when they come. People with low self-esteem have a hindering tendency to focus on their shortcomings. If you are doubtful about the validity of your accomplishment, ask a highly trusted individual if they think it means anything. You want to surround yourself with positive people. Doing so will allow you and your friends and loved ones to revel in successes.

The key to this strategy is acknowledging progress. For example, if you are trying to learn an unfamiliar foreign language, congratulate yourself when you memorize and internalize a new word or grammatical concept. Do not wallow over the words that you have not learned; that will make you overwhelmed and likely to give up. Most people do not even know every word of their native language. Your successes, small and large, deserve recognition and celebration. Treat success as something worth acknowledging and you will find yourself with incredible self-esteem and confidence.

On the other hand, do not linger on any one success for too long. If you have the world in your hands, it can slip through your fingers if you let go of it in order to pat yourself on the back. However, your strengths and positive attributes contribute to your success. So, by recognizing your own successes, you in turn give credibility and validity to your perceived strengths.

Identify Your Unique Strengths

Chances are, you possess many strengths. Sadly, people who suffer from self-esteem issues have trouble believing in their own positive traits. Realistically, no one person is strong (or weak) at everything in life. Everybody possesses their own unique strengths. So, stop measuring yourself against your peers. Activities that your neighbor excels at may give you trouble, and vice versa. In order to boost your own self-esteem, focus on your own strengths instead of the next person's. You likely have a wealth of skills, achievements, positive traits, and experiences to be proud of. Start identifying them.

First, identify your strongest skills. Try to write a list of ten (or more) skills that you possess. These skills do not need to be spectacular, world-changing abilities. For example, maybe you are great at keeping your home tidy. Perhaps you possess superb writing, cooking, or communicating skills. Craft a ten-item long list that outlines your best skills. Make sure that this does not turn into an exercise in self-loathing; do not include things like "ruining my life" on your list.

Next, identify your biggest achievements. People with self-esteem problems have a hard time recognizing their own accomplishments. You should not take your achievements for granted. Recognize the hard work and dedication that went into your best accomplishments. For example, maybe you are proud of how you moved out of your parents' home and got a place of your own. Even graduating from high school is not an easy feat. Because of the constant demands that society places on people trying to achieve, many individuals take their hard work for granted. There is this underlying belief that hard work should not be celebrated because of the fact that it is simply expected. However, if you fail to recognize your own hard work, you stand to achieve without being proud of your accomplishments. That will not improve your self-esteem. Try crafting a list of at least five achievements of which you are proud. This exercise will help you realize your potential and encourage you to pursue greater accomplishments in the future. Additional examples of possible items for this list include graduating college, paying off debt, starring in a commercial, winning a championship, and having a child.

Next, look at past experiences where you overcame adversity. Studies demonstrate that people who have overcome adversity and are consciously aware of it possess higher levels of happiness. This exercise will help you discover your ability to cope with hardships. Craft a list of three or more times in which you willingly overcame adversity. For each list item, jot down a detailed summary of the adversity in question along with the skills and strengths that helped you overcome it. For example, perhaps you dislocated your elbow and had to take up a second job for a year to pay off hospital bills. In this situation, you used your work ethic and grit to overcome debts. This is only an example, however. List situations relevant to your life.

Recognize Loved Ones

Loved ones have a profound impact on self-esteem. From an early age, you receive messages from the people who care about you that affect the ways in which you value yourself. Some hurt your self-esteem; others help it. In any case, focusing on the people who value you the most will help you realize your value as a person. So, think about the people who have helped you in the past and the people who you have helped as well.

The people who have helped you in the past did so because they value you. If your life was worthless, nobody would find it worthwhile to help you. Go beyond identifying the people who helped you. Come up with a list of five detailed experiences you had in which people went out of their way to assist you. Perhaps your parent helped you pay off a personal debt.

Maybe a promoter went out of his way to highlight your work. In any case, people help you because they feel like you are worth helping. Taking the time to consciously make yourself aware of this fact will change the way that you see yourself for the better. Also, you do not have to stop at five list items. If you can come up with more, then you should.

Conversely, try to identify five times in which you went out of your way to help another person. Again, detailed accounts are necessary for this exercise to work as well as it can. When you help another person, the person whom you helped will value you for your selflessness. When you recall details regarding occasions on which you selflessly assisted another person, you give value to your actions. Your activity improved the life of another human being. That in and of itself is something to be proud of. Your actions make a difference in other people's lives.

Practice Gratitude

Gratitude is the act of consciously giving appreciation to the positive things in your own life. Gratitude can relate to the present, future, or past. Of course, if you have a good thing in your life right now, give thanks for it. You can also be thankful for the future possibilities that lie ahead. Additionally, even if a great thing or person is no longer in your life, you can still be grateful for the fact that they were in your life at all. For example, if you have lost a loved one, nothing is stopping you from practicing gratitude towards the time and experiences that you got to share with them in the past. They were a part of your journey through life, and that is more than enough to be thankful for.

Life owes us nothing, so anything positive that does come into one's life should be cherished and appreciated. For a beginning exercise in gratitude, craft an itemized list of fifty things, people, events, occasions, pets, and experiences that you feel thankful for. If you have trouble, think about circumstances that have had a meaningful impact on your life. Chances are, you can find something to be grateful for regarding impactful happenings.

Realizing that you have at least dozens of things to be thankful for will raise your self-esteem and make you feel better about life in general. A positive outlook will contribute to a more positive idea about oneself.

Chapter 3: Step 3 – Love Yourself

If you love your dog, you will nurture and care for your pet. You will feed him or her a healthy diet, avoid neglecting them, praise them for good behavior, take them to the experts at the veterinarian's office when they fall ill, ensure their overall health, and foster healthy, socially acceptable behavior through the use of positive reinforcement training methods. Similarly, if you love yourself, you will take care of your social, physical, mental, and spiritual health. This chapter will show you practical strategies that you can implement in order to practice loving yourself.

Feed Yourself a Healthy Diet

Self-esteem issues harm those who suffer from them. Some people with low self-esteem will overindulge in unhealthy menu items because they do not believe that they are worthy of the efforts required to maintain a healthy diet. However, people who love themselves take care of their bodies and minds. One's diet is one of the biggest predictors of their health. People with high self-esteem take care of themselves in the form of eating a healthy diet.

This is not a book on dieting, so it will not go into great detail regarding what you should and should not eat. No two people have precisely the same Calorie and nutrition needs. Instead, this section will largely cover the benefits that a healthy diet will breed and how they contribute to high levels of self-esteem.

Food affects mood. This is not new science. As such, you should try to build a balanced diet around menu items that are proven to enhance humans' moods. These include foods with high amounts of serotonin-producing carbohydrates, selenium, vitamin D, omega-3 fatty acids, and vitamin B. They affect the brain in such a way that make their consumers experience pleasant long-term feelings. Feeling good in general is one way to boost self-esteem.

In addition, people who eat better have more attractive, fitter bodies. When you look better in the mirror, you will feel better about yourself. A healthier body will lend itself to raises in self-esteem. Furthermore, you will feel better about your choices, eliminating the hampering guilt that comes along with poor diet selections.

Eat a balanced diet that contains minimal amounts of caffeine, alcohol, and added sugars. These substances worsen moods in the long-term. Caffeine consumption leads to mood swings and crashes. Alcohol consumption causes feelings of sluggishness, irritability, and anxiety once its intoxicating effects wear off. And, added sugars damage health and contribute to weight problems. If you want to feel good about yourself, you need to dedicate yourself to a healthy eating plan.

Keep Yourself Fit

Physical exercise is a great way to boost self-esteem. As long as you are able-bodied enough, you should strive to get regular vigorous physical activity, at least twenty minutes daily. Exercise makes the brain shoot off endorphins that boost mood. Furthermore, your body will look better as you increase your fitness levels. Looking good contributes to self-esteem. Also, you will feel good about your choice to engage in physical exercise. That rewarding feeling will serve to further motivate you to continue making your good choices.

In addition, certain exercises provide people with concrete validations of their achievements and improvements. For example, a weightlifter will know when he or she becomes stronger; they will be able to lift heavier reps. When you start adding more weight to your reps, you will have tangible proof of your increased weightlifting abilities. Such an accomplishment will contribute to the building of your self-esteem. Furthermore, runners will feel good about their accomplishments when they shave seconds off of their times.

However, exercise's benefits extend past those related to cosmetic appearances, physical fitness, and pride associated with improvements in abilities. Any time that you make a choice that causes you to get healthier, your self-esteem will increase. People who love themselves choose to keep themselves healthy.

Forgive Yourself

Every living human makes regrettable mistakes. The key, then, to healthy self-esteem lies not within avoiding mistakes, but in how you choose to handle them. When you err, accept that it is okay to live imperfectly. You do not have to be your absolute best at all times. In fact, a perfectionist attitude can be unattractive and damaging.

Additionally, when you are able to forgive yourself for merely having faults and flaws, you will develop the ability to forgive other people for theirs. If you are able to move past the imperfect behaviors of others, you will live a much happier life. On the other hand, if you victimize yourself by blaming the actions of others for your shortcomings and unhappiness, you place that situation out of your control. Forgiveness and understanding are essential elements of becoming the leader of your own life. Forgive everyone, including yourself!

When you do make a mistake that you wish you had not committed, do not beat yourself up over it. Calling yourself names and assigning negative attributes such as "stupid" and "incapable" to yourself damages your self-esteem greatly. Do not diminish your own self-worth. Instead, figure out how you can improve yourself in order to avoid making the same mistake again. For example, if you unknowingly make a post on social media that contains implied racism, apologize for your mistake and consider taking a class on cultural sensitivity.

Utilize Therapy

If your self-esteem issues appear beyond your control, consider attending therapy sessions with a qualified therapist. Therapists are professionally trained to help individuals with issues relating to self-esteem. A therapist's couch can provide the perfect judgement-free zone and professional that will help you move past issues that hamper self-esteem. You will be listened to and helped. Making use of this service requires that you open up and make your story known to the therapist, so be ready to share. You have to want to help yourself, but that is probably why you picked up this book.

Get Checked

Loving oneself involves actively maintaining the physical and mental elements of the human form. Practice self-love by allowing professionals to ensure that you are functioning optimally. For example, get a dental checkup every year; have a physician examine you regularly; if you feel like it might benefit you, get yourself a psychological evaluation. Not only will you benefit from the fixes that the professionals give you, you will also feel good about yourself knowing that you took steps to ensure that everything is okay with your body and mind. You will feel at ease when you have the knowledge that any potential problems are being tended to by qualified professionals. Do not let your health, physical, dental, mental, or otherwise, go neglected. You deserve to live life in optimum condition.

Sleep Well

Part of caring for yourself involves ensuring that you get plenty of restful sleep. It is not a secret that sleep deprivation can lead to problems with physical, emotional, and mental health. However, more recent research suggests that poor sleep habits can harm one's self-esteem.

Sleep deprivation hampers your ability to cope with stress. In fact, some people deal with stress by taking a nap. Sleep benefits humans greatly, so that is one of the healthiest ways to cope with the stressors of the modern world. Still, the demands of Western culture's productivity-oriented society make it very difficult for large numbers of people to obtain sleep when they need it the most.

The link between sleep deprivation and reduced self-esteem is astounding. When you fail to sleep well, you have a much harder time handling stressors than you do when you are well-rested. You feel more sensitive, get irritated more easily, and have a tough time managing relationships appropriately.

Feelings of sensitivity manifest themselves in those who do not sleep well. For example, imagine that you are chatting with a friend online, and they suddenly stop responding. Their status displays that they are still connected, so their failure to reply might make you not only frustrated, but fearful that you have said something to make them not want to talk to you. Sleep deprivation increases this feeling of fearfulness as your mind is likely not sharp enough to consider all possible reasons why your friend is not responding. The self-doubt that this situation causes will lead to drops in self-esteem.

Next, humans are more irritable when they are sleep deprived. In other words, sleep deprived people experience reduced levels of patience for others. When you impatiently interact with others, they will subconsciously give off feedback that informs you of their disliking of your attitude. Receiving negative feedback like this can hurt your self-esteem, unless you are rested and therefore mentally sharp enough to recognize that such reactions indicate a need to change your approach. Furthermore, you might find yourself upset with yourself about the way that you handle inconveniences while sleep deprived. Sleep deprivation also amplifies the hindering effects of many mental health issues, including depression.

Finally, sleep deprivation contributes to strained interpersonal relationships. What would be a minor annoyance from another person while you are fully rested takes the form of an amplified source of frustration when you are not running on sufficient sleep. As such, sleep deprivation can cause you to regard other people with frustration, which in turn causes you to push them away. Strained relationships can seriously damage one's self-esteem.

In order to get a good night's sleep, you can perform certain activities that will promote healthy sleep habits. Start by taking regular breaks from working. Working hard breeds success, but short breaks of five to ten minutes every now and then during the workday will help your brain relax enough to fall asleep at night. In addition, practicing mindfulness meditation during the day has been shown to assist with restful sleep. Make sure that your sleeping quarters or bedroom is dark and cool; our tribal ancestors had no choice but to sleep in those conditions, so get in touch with your roots. Before you sleep, spend an hour or so just unwinding; do not use stimulating devices like television, tablets, and smartphones. The stimulation that they provide combined with the light that they radiate will impede on your sleep. Obviously, avoid stimulants like cocaine and caffeine during the second half of your day, as they hamper the body's ability to fall asleep. And, if you find yourself worrying about keeping track of upcoming responsibilities and obligations, keep stationery and a writing utensil near your bed so that you can write down to-dos and not have to mentally track them.

Lastly, a regular, consistent sleep schedule is preferred over irregular sleep patterns. So, try to get a solid night's sleep each night. Some people make the mistake of running on insufficient sleep during the work week, and then spending the weekend catching up, often spending ten to twelve hours asleep on Friday and Saturday nights. Instead, aim to obtain enough sleep every night. Keeping a consistent sleep schedule will prevent you from having to adjust when Monday comes.

Chapter 4: Step 4 - Assert Yourself

People with low self-esteem believe that other people will have an easy time taking a disliking to them. As such, they avoid asserting themselves lest another person start to dislike them for their assertions. Low self-esteem individuals would rather blend in and go with the flow than stand out and potentially cause a riff. As a result, low self-esteem individuals usually end up sacrificing their own needs for the sake of staying unnoticed and not disliked. This ultimately leads to further drops in self-esteem as the right to voice one's own needs goes unexercised. People will feel guilty and weak about not expressing their own needs.

On the other hand, people who assert themselves have been proven to have higher self-esteem than those who do not. Asserting yourself is a surefire way to build a solid foundation of self-esteem. Remember that people with high self-esteem are better at leading their own lives.

Challenge Yourself

When you undertake a new challenge, you exit your comfort zone. You leave a life of complacency in exchange for moments of uncertainty. Uncertainty feels uncomfortable, but you will never grow if you fail to challenge yourself. Build self-esteem by taking up a challenge. You might get involved with a new hobby or take up a sport that you are unfamiliar with. The experience itself is worthwhile, but its side effects stand to change the person that you think you are.

Even if you fail at your self-imposed challenge, you can feel good about trying. If you like your newfound activity, you might even practice it and attempt to get better. Challenging yourself to do something that you are wholly unfamiliar with will expand your horizons. So, consider learning an instrument, studying a language, or attempting an athletic feat.

You might also challenge yourself to improve the quality of your life. You can challenge yourself to find a better job, move to a better home, or save up a sufficient sum of money that will pay for a down payment on that home. In any case, challenge yourself; you will grow as a person.

Stand Up for Yourself

Some people will go out of their way to appease others because they feel that that is the only way to make others like them. This faulty reasoning can lead to others walking all over them. If you stretch your capabilities in an effort to get other people to like you, then you stand to let them take advantage of you and your talents. Standing up for yourself is an assertive process that requires saying "no" at the right times, setting boundaries, and establishing control over your choices.

First, learning to say the word "no" can do wonders for your self-esteem. This is not to suggest that you should power trip all over yourself and negate people at every opportunity. Rather, if somebody else's request will place undue hardship on you at the moment, feel free to decline their plea for assistance. Unless the situation in question is an emergency or has highly urgent implications, you are under no obligation to go out of your way for somebody else. Of course, you should return favors when you can, but not at the expense of your own well-being.

For example, imagine that you are a full-time student working part time. Your boss asks if you can cover a shift tomorrow, during which time you were planning on completing a lengthy essay for one of your college classes. You had already set aside that specific timeframe in order to dedicate yourself to this paper. If you agree to work, you will be hard pressed to find an alternate time to finish the school assignment. You can tell your boss that you will be there, but then you stand to fall behind in your coursework. Instead, understand that you have every right to tell your boss that you are too busy to work. If your boss really needed you so badly, then he or she should have scheduled you for that shift further in advance. You do not have to provide the solutions to everybody's problems.

Second, setting boundaries will do wonders for your self-esteem. You are worthy enough to decide what you are comfortable with and not let anyone else make that decision for you. For example, if your coworker greets you with a hug every day, and that makes you uncomfortable, set boundaries by asking him not to hug you in the future. In your coworker's case, the polite thing to do would be to respect your boundaries and keep his hands off of you. You have the right to establish the limits of your relationships.

Of course, setting boundaries might be uncomfortable at first. Your hugging coworker might take personal offense to the fact that his touch makes you uncomfortable. If this happens, you can ease tensions by explaining that you believe that hugging between coworkers is not appropriate for the workplace. Make sure to establish that your boundaries are a matter of personal principle, rather than specific to any one person. You do not have to let anybody do something to you that you do not want them to do in order for them to like you. In fact, people will likely respect you more when you set boundaries appropriately.

Keep your boundaries reasonable. For example, if a friendly, harmless coworker greets you with a smile and a "good morning," it would be inappropriate to snap at him with a phrase like "do not talk to me." Setting boundaries does not equate to being standoffish.

Third, you should make efforts to establish control over your choices. Your life is in your hands now, so act accordingly. (Of course, exceptions do exist – if you are underage, your parents have the right to make decisions for you. If you are incarcerated, your guards make a lot of choices for you, for example.) Make decisions and stand by them.

For example, if you are about to go off to college, do not let distant relatives tell you what to study (unless they are helping you pay tuition; then, you might want to appease them). If you want to take up a job in a new city, then you have the autonomy and freedom to decide to move and accept that position. You are not tied down by invisible forces.

Assertiveness vs. Aggressiveness

Unfortunately, assertiveness and aggressiveness are often confused with one another. Somewhat similar in nature, these behaviors tend to cloud one another as individuals struggle to distinguish between them. A fine line lies in between them. For our purposes, assertiveness is desired while aggressiveness is frowned upon and to be minimized or avoided.

Aggressiveness takes the form of domination in attempts at winning. If an aggressor wins, then somebody else loses. Aggressors do not take into consideration the feelings, needs, autonomy, rights, or desires of others. They try to get what they want without regard for their fellow humans. An example of aggressive behavior would be if a boss makes an employee stay later than they were scheduled to and finish a gigantic pile of tasks, lest that employee lose their job. The boss gets what he needs – a completed workload – but does so at the expense and well-being of his unfortunate employee. He had no regard for his subordinate, and thus behaved aggressively. Some might even say that the boss abused his authority in this situation.

On the other hand, assertive behavior involves articulating one's own needs, desires, and wants while simultaneously exercising consideration for other people. If the boss in the above example had chosen to behave assertively, he would have gone about the situation much differently. An assertive boss would have gathered his staff, informed them about the workload that needed to be completed, and asked that they divide up the tasks and prioritize them during the employees' respective shifts. The boss still gets what he needs, but works with his team in order to ensure that their needs are accounted for.

Furthermore, the boss in this example could also behave in a nonassertive, nonaggressive manner, avoiding giving out the workload at all. However, that would not be productive for anybody involved. Assertiveness should be valued over aggressiveness. Assertive behavior involves strategizing and cooperating with others in order to ensure that everybody is treated fairly while getting what they need.

Assertiveness does not involve bullying, threatening, or intimidating. Rather, it involves communicating with and considering others.

How to Develop an Assertive Personality
By now, this chapter has covered concrete tactics that will improve your assertiveness and methods for differentiating between aggressiveness and assertiveness. However, assertiveness can and should be internalized. A high level of

self-esteem will manifest itself in an assertive personality, and vice versa. In this section, you will learn the changes that you can make to your mindset and habits that will lead to an overall increase in assertiveness. In addition, assertiveness will start to come naturally and comfortably once you make these practices become habits.

First, you must express your ideas, thoughts, and feelings in such a way that is positive and healthy. You might be very angry over a situation, but that does not give you the right to lash out at others; snapping out of anger is aggressive, not assertive. Do confront those who infringe on your rights and well-being, but do so in a respectful, emotionally controlled manner. For example, imagine that you are frustrated with your roommate because he hardly ever cleans up after himself. You might be very tempted to call him lazy and shout at him about his tidiness habits; in fact, you might even feel justified in doing so. However, those behaviors demonstrate aggressiveness. Instead, you should calmly explain that you feel frustrated at his lack of effort and need more out of him in terms of keeping clean. You might even want to detail the reasons why keeping shared spaces tidy is important to you.

Second, place importance on your rights as a person. Understand and believe that your feelings, rights, emotions, desires, thoughts, and needs are equally as valuable as everyone else's. You are no more or less valuable than is the next person. Do not make apologies for expressing your ideas or acting in your own best interest. You deserve the best that you can provide for yourself, and so does everybody else. Just make sure that your successes do not come at the expense of another person or animal. Similarly, do not let other people take advantage of you in order to further their own agendas.

Thirdly, handle both compliments and constructive criticism appropriately. When you receive a compliment, understand that you have earned it. People with low self-esteem have a hard time accepting compliments because of the fact that they do not believe that they are praiseworthy. Hardly anyone, if anybody at all, will give out compliments sarcastically. Say "thank you" to somebody when they reward your efforts or talents with a compliment.

On the other hand, you may find yourself on the receiving end of constructive criticism that you never really asked for. If somebody has your best interests in mind, they will give you constructive criticism because they truly have a desire to see you succeed and better yourself and your work. You have every right to disagree with criticism; however, take care to avoid becoming defensive or upset. If you do not want to further entertain criticism, you can still handle it well by smiling and saying something to the effect of "Well, thank you for the suggestion."

Also, you can make the most out of criticism by asking for further advice relating to your work. For example, imagine that you have turned in a report to your boss. Your boss then informs you that, next time, you should focus more on your introductory paragraph. You can ask for specifics regarding how to improve it, such as where you should put your thesis statement. People with high self-esteem are ever-curious about how they can improve; they do not view criticism as a reflection of their self-worth.

Fourth, realize that you have little to no control over the reactionary behavior of others. Some people simply respond poorly to assertive behavior. They might get upset with you for sticking up for yourself. Remember, however, that your goal does not involve getting trampled on in order to appease others and make them fond of you. Your goal is to build your self-esteem and take control of your own life.

So, if somebody has a problem with your assertiveness, it is probably a reflection of their own insecurities. Insecure people, namely those with low self-esteem, will try to prevent others from bettering themselves so that they might remain equal. So long as you are respectful and not infringing on another person's rights or needs, then you possess every right to do as you please. You cannot help it if your peer fails to respect you and your needs. Cut these problematic insecure people out of your life and move on.

Finally, speak up for yourself. If your needs are not being met, do or say something about it and keep speaking until your needs get the attention that they deserve. This might mean that you have to take it upon yourself to fulfill your own needs, but you deserve to do so. If your needs are unfulfilled, you will have an extremely difficult time achieving your fullest potential. For example, you cannot work as hard as you possibly can if you are not being granted your lawfully owed lunch breaks at work. Unfortunately, you cannot depend on another person to recognize that your needs are not being met. In most cases, you will have to go out of your way and call attention to yourself in order to get what you rightfully deserve. For example, you might have to talk to your company's human resources department if you are not getting to take deserved lunch breaks. At the same time, you must ensure that you meet your needs without belittling or sacrificing the well-being of other people in the process.

Assertive Wording

The ways in which you phrase your expressions, thoughts, and requests can make a world of difference regarding how other people perceive your statements. Specific wording will allow you to communicate your needs, desires, and wants without offending or seemingly blaming anybody else. These phrasing tactics were developed through years of thorough communication research.

First, make use of "I statements." "I statements" are sentences that put emphasis on your feelings about a situation, rather than cast blame on your conversation partner. For example, you should say "I feel frustrated when you..." instead of "You frustrate me when...." By focusing the conversation on yourself, you will allow your conversation partner to relax as they realize that the issue is about your emotions rather than their flaws and faults.

Second, the verbs that you use when speaking can alter the other person's perceptions of your message. Experts recommend using "won't" in place of "can't," "could" in place of "should," "choose to" in place of "have to," and "want" in place of "need." The preferred verbs place control and power in your hands. The verbs to be avoided convey weakness, lack of power, and an unwillingness to act assertively.

For example, consider the "won't" vs. "can't" theory. If you say "I won't eat pickles," you convey that you have a choice in the matter. That sentence implies that you could eat them if you wanted to, but you prefer not to, so you won't. On the other hand, stating "I can't eat pickles" implies that you have a literal inability to consume a certain food. This could prompt others to try to convince you to eat one as they attempt to make you believe in your abilities more. "I won't" implies strength and conviction.

Communicating Assertively

In addition to wording and phrasing schemes, certain communication behaviors can be used in order to assertively assert yourself. Communication scholars generally agree that certain communication tactics are more effective, assertive, and respectful than others. This section will detail the best general techniques for engaging in assertive communication with others.

First, empathy is a great tool for easing the tensions that assertive communication sometimes creates. At its core, empathy is the conscious recognition of another person's thoughts and emotions. Communicate your empathy, and then state your request. In the case of an untidy roommate, you might do this by saying "I get that you feel overwhelmed with school and work. However, I need you to take no more than fifteen minutes each night to make sure that your dishes are washed and your trash is discarded."

Next, you can put the broken record tactic to use when another person does not seem to understand the seriousness of your message. For example, if your classmate asks you for a ride to the next town over, and obliging them would put a genuine strain on your time, politely inform them of that fact until they take it seriously. Word your responses identically each time. Such a conversation might play out like this:

Classmate: *Hey, do you think you could give me ride to Eureka later this afternoon?*

You: *Sorry, I have to work on a project for public speaking class.*

Classmate: *I can offer you ten dollars.*

You: *I have to work on a project for public speaking class.*

Classmate: *For real though, I have to get to Eureka by 5:00.*

You: *I have to work on a project for public speaking class.*

Classmate: *Please, it would really help me out. I am asking as a personal favor.*

You: *I'm sorry, and I do value you as a friend, but I really have to work on a project for public speaking class.*

You can and should vary the tones of your responses, but try to keep the words that you use fairly consistent and identical. Like a broken record replays the same segment of a song over and over, keep repeating yourself unrelentingly until the other person involved in the conversation grasps the gravity of your words. When they realize that you mean what you say, they might get embarrassed over the fact that they kept pressing you when you clearly could not help them out. Hopefully, they learn from the experience and respect your time better in the future.

Moving along, the escalation technique makes itself useful when your requests are not initially fulfilled. Keeping respect and assertiveness in mind, this tactic involves establishing firmer and firmer consequences until your needs are met. For example, if you are not getting your rightfully owed lunch breaks at work, talk to your boss about it. If your boss does not resolve the issue, tell him that you will speak to the human resources branch of your workplace. If you have to follow through and go to human resources, hopefully they can help you. In the event that the human resources division does not produce a satisfactory resolution, you might escalate by threatening to get a lawyer involved. Keep escalating assertively until you get what you deserve.

Next, you sometimes need extra time to respond to another person. If you find yourself unsure of the response that you want to give, you have every right to inform the other person that you need time to consider their offer or request. For example, you might respond to a request for help with a statement like "I am not entirely sure if I have the time to do that for you right now. Let me check my schedule and get back to you in fifteen minutes." If the other person has any respect for your time, they will say okay and trust you to follow through. Of course, always uphold your word and respond when you say you will, even if just to inform the other person that you need more time than you originally said you would.

Finally, scripting comes in handy when you want to premeditate your assertive conversational approach. Scripting involves crafting a prepared approach that contains four components: the situation, your emotions, your needs, and the desired outcome.

The situation component contains a description of your viewpoint concerning the event. For example, "Professor, you gave us two days to turn in a twelve-page essay. This was not noted anywhere in the syllabus, which means that many of my classmates and I are struggling to finish the assignment on time."

Your emotions regarding the situation should be made known: "This is causing a lot of us extreme amounts of anxiety and stress."

You must clearly articulate your needs: "I need you to extend the deadline for this assignment and give us more advanced notice for big assignments in the future."

And, you have to state the outcome that will result should the other person fulfill your needs: "I want to succeed in your class. If you allow more time for this assignment, then I will be abler to produce a well-composed paper."

Chapter 5: Step 5 – Stop Hurting Your Self-Esteem

Certain behaviors are known to lower self-esteem within those who practice them. This chapter is designed to give readers a list of actions that must be avoided if self-esteem is to be built.

Living Amongst Clutter

Clutter accumulates when you fail to organize or tidy up your surroundings in a timely manner. It looks messy and implies a lack of willpower. The cause of clutter can be traced to an inability to admit to poor decisions. When you buy something that you have no practical use for, it sits in your home, vehicle, or office and takes up space without possessing any real utility. It becomes clutter when you cannot admit to yourself that buying that item was a mistake. Clutter builds up when you cannot bring yourself to get rid of or properly file away unneeded possessions or documents. Clutter can be tangible, such as when you sloppily pile papers on top of one another. It can also be digital; undeleted unimportant emails can make your inbox cluttered. In any case, living amongst clutter will hurt anyone's self-esteem.

Furthermore, simply touching a frivolous item can increase the likelihood that it turns to clutter. Studies demonstrate that touching any object will likely cause you to develop an emotional sense of attachment to that item. This is the reason why famous retailers encourage shoppers to touch the products in the store. Apple Computers lets potential customers use their devices from the confines of the Apple store at no cost. Cell phone retailers let shoppers handle and interact with the various cell phone models that they offer.

Clothing shops allow customers to try on outfits before going through with their purchase. So, if you touch an object for a period of time, you will have a harder time getting rid of it and thus eliminating clutter.

Unfortunately, clutter's effects on the human psyche are hampering. Research proves that clutter raises stress, overstimulates senses, and hampers the ability to focus within those who live and work amongst it. As a result, clutter will make you feel worse about yourself.

To deal with clutter, do not overwhelm yourself. If your clutter piles are especially large, you might have a hard time confronting them all at once. Instead, dedicate a predetermined block of time to each cluttered area in your life. Aim to spend thirty minutes on your inbox, another thirty on your closet, and so on. Work diligently, but once that half hour expires, you are done for the day with that particular location. Clutter builds because dealing with it is hard. If you strive to deal with an entire pile at once, you stand to develop feelings of overwhelm.

Procrastinating

Adults with healthy self-esteem do their best to take care of nagging tasks in a timely manner. You might get a sense of dread when you look at the bills that make their way into your mailbox, but letting them linger unpaid will harm your self-esteem. Waiting until the final possible moment to handle menial tasks will cause stress and undue anxiety. Handle your business as soon as you can, and you will feel better about yourself.

To illustrate, wash your dishes as soon as you are done eating; pay your bills as soon as you accumulate the money for them; wash your unclean laundry before you run out of garments to wear; fill up your vehicle's gasoline tank before you have to wonder whether you will have enough time or gasoline to make it to your next destination; respond to urgent emails immediately. You will only make your life harder in the future if you avoid your responsibilities in the moment. If your life becomes more difficult than it needs to be because of poor choices that you made, you will feel unsatisfied with your ability to manage your own life. In turn, your self-esteem will diminish. Do not let that happen.

Living Like a Child

Maybe you miss the days of your childhood in which you had very little responsibility compared to adulthood. Some people make every attempt to relive those days by failing to live like an adult. Even if you feel that you are owed a childhood-like existence because of missed experiences, you cannot go through life living like a child. Doing so will only reinforce the idea that you cannot handle adulthood properly.

Basically, living like an adult means taking initiative and avoiding childish behavior. Initiative requires that you take it upon yourself to figure out how to serve your own best interests, and then taking those actions. Such actions include setting up plans for the future, handling money responsibly, cleaning up after yourself, and practicing kind manners. On the other hand, childish behaviors include living hedonistically, wasting money, leaving messes behind, and behaving rudely.

First, adult-like initiative involves setting up plans that will improve your life. For example, set up regular dental cleanings that will improve your oral hygiene. The childish counterpart to this behavior is a completely hedonistic approach to life. Hedonism is pleasure-seeking. For many people, a visit to the dentist is not a source of pleasure, so a full-on hedonist will not book themselves a dental appointment. As a result, their self-esteem will fall as they fail to maintain a healthy mouth.

Second, an adult-like lifestyle involves the responsible handling of money. If you do not want to live like a child, stop splurging on possessions that you should not spend money on. (Of course, if you have loads of money to spare, enjoy yourself.) If you use your limited funds responsibly, you will develop a greater control over your own life. So, instead of splurging twenty-five dollars on a pizza delivery, for example, see if you can make the same dish at home for a very small portion of the delivery service's menu price.

Third, if you want to live like an adult, clean your messes. Childlike individuals do not understand the value of a clean dwelling. Furthermore, a messy home indicates an inability to care for oneself. Your unclean environment will provide you with a reflection of your lack of willpower, which will reduce your self-esteem. Wash your dishes, make your bed, and so forth. Keep clean, and stop leaving messes behind.

Lastly, practice politeness. Manners indicate healthy self-esteem. When you practice good manners genuinely, most people whom you interact with will respond positively to your polite attitude. As a result, you will benefit from this feedback; your self-esteem will increase. Conversely, when you behave rudely, other people will regard you with disdain and may even go out of their way to avoid you. The negative attitudes that these people develop towards you will affect your self-esteem in a harmful way when you realize how they feel about you. Your behavior affects how others see you, which affects how you see yourself. Practice basic respect for others and you will have an easier time feeling great about yourself.

Avoiding Other People

Dealing with people effectively boosts self-esteem. For example, if you call your mom back as soon as you get her voicemail, you will feel good about your ability to return phone calls. In addition, the anxiety and stress that would have otherwise been caused by the obligation to return her call will not affect you for long. When you avoid interactions with other people, you are not doing yourself any favors. Interpersonal interactions are an unavoidable part of our society. The sooner that you deal with your fellow human beings, the more self-esteem you stand to retain. If you put off an inevitable interaction long enough, you might even start to doubt your ability to deal with it; that cannot be beneficial for your self-esteem.

Intoxicants

Alcohol use and abuse are closely linked to low self-esteem. Low self-esteem contributes to alcohol abuse, and alcohol abuse leads to low self-esteem. The result comes in the form of a downward spiral called addiction. Many people with low self-esteem turn to alcohol because it provides them with temporary relief from the unpleasant feelings that their low self-esteem causes.

Unfortunately, the pleasantness of intoxication wears off. Once it does, alcohol abusers are left with even worse feelings about themselves, which makes them want to drink again in order to escape their misery. This strategy rarely works in the long run. If you find yourself turning to alcohol or other dangerous drugs to cope with self-esteem issues, consult with a professional to determine if you should seek addiction treatment.

Once alcohol abusers learn to deal with their personal issues in healthier ways, their lives improve drastically. Quitting a bad alcohol habit will improve one's physical health, cognitive functions, outlook on life, relationships, coping skills, and, perhaps most importantly, self-esteem.

In addition to alcohol, individuals suffering with low self-esteem sometimes turn to other harmful drugs as a way to deal with negative emotions. This unhealthy practice can also lead to addiction. For some, willpower is enough to overcome such a harmful coping mechanism. For others, professional treatment programs are necessary. In any case, turning to drugs when you feel poorly about yourself will only damage your self-esteem in the long run.

Conclusion

Thank for making it through to the end of *Leadership and self-deception: Maximise your potential for a successful life in 5 Steps*. I hope that you found it informative and able to provide you with all of the tools you need to achieve your self-esteem building and life leading goals, whatever those might be.

The next step is to actively practice the suggestions, tactics, and techniques found in the pages of this book. In chapter 1, you learned the importance of having self-esteem. Chapter 2 taught you about the power of positivity. You learned concrete techniques for caring for and loving yourself in chapter 3. Chapter 4 detailed appropriate assertiveness strategies. The final chapter outlined mistakes that harm self-esteem that you should take care to avoid. In just 5 steps, you can build a healthy foundation of self-esteem that will improve the quality of your life and make you more attractive.

It is my hope that you lead your own life and refuse to let unwanted sources of authority make decisions for you.

Finally, if you found this book useful in anyway, a review on Amazon is always appreciated! Happy leading!

About the Author

Thomas Garry is a passionate entrepreneur, author, and motivational speaker who currently resides in Perth, Western Australia.

Starting out, Thomas worked as a salesman in the technology industry and dabbled in network marketing. After years of extensive studying and soul-searching, he decided to work for himself and become an entrepreneur. Nearly a decade later, Thomas had to make the difficult decision to close his company. This failure ultimately served as his driving force.

Today, Thomas is infinitely dedicated to providing people with the tools necessary to unleash their limitless potential so that they can achieve their goals. Through his motivational methods, he teaches others to face challenges head on so that they can finally live the life that they have always dreamed of.

Thomas Garry has been happily married for 20 years and is the proud father of two sons.

"Nothing binds you except your thoughts; nothing limits you except your fear; and nothing controls you except your beliefs. Everything is within you."
-Marianne Williamson

www.ingramcontent.com/pod-product-compliance
Lightning Source LLC
Chambersburg PA
CBHW061224180526
45170CB00003B/1149